ICONIC AMERICA

NEW YORK CITY

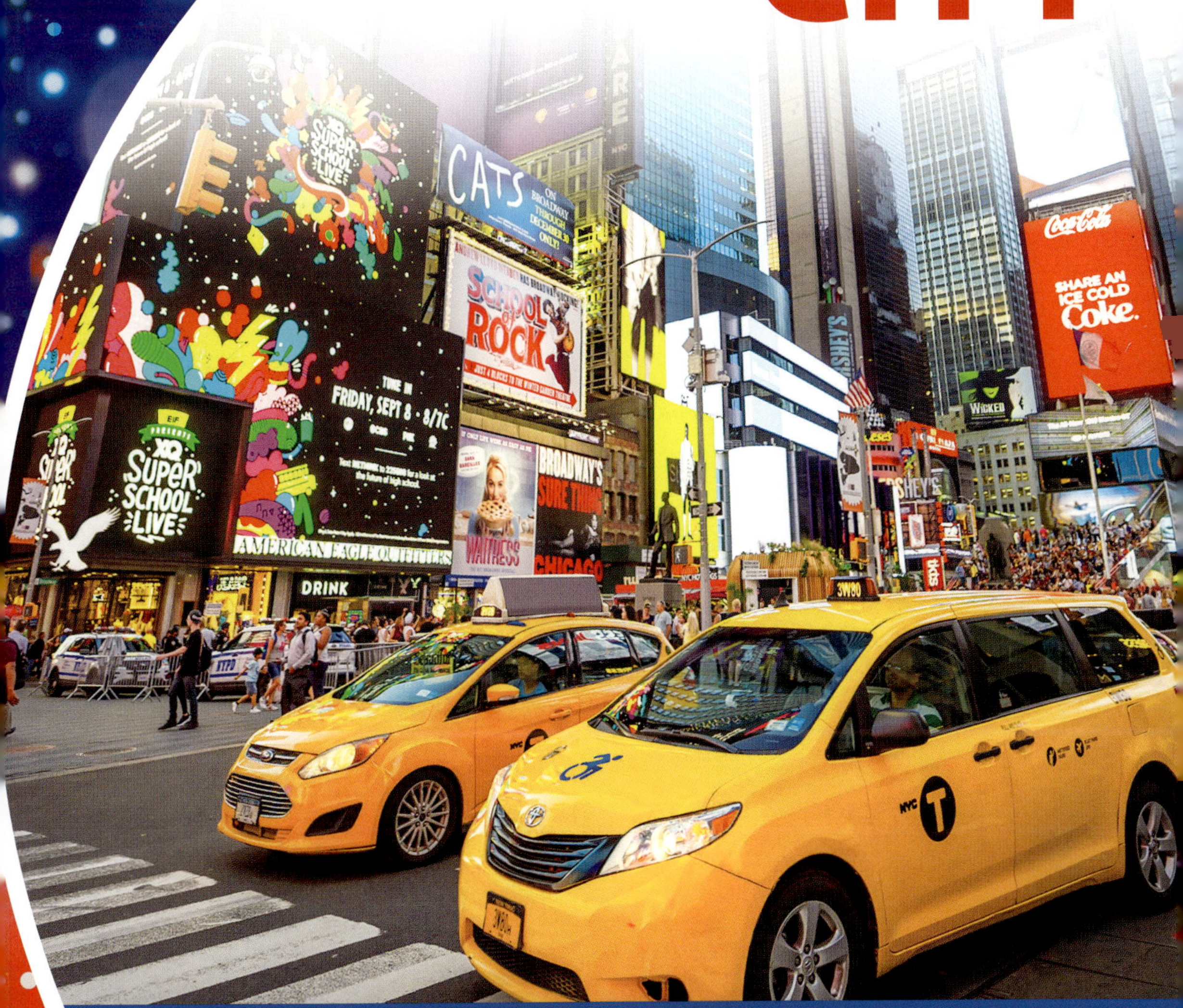

BY MARNE VENTURA

CONTENT CONSULTANT
Reuben Rose-Redwood, PhD
Associate Professor of Geography
University of Victoria

Cover image: Billboards advertise plays and other attractions in New York City's Times Square.

An Imprint of Abdo Publishing
abdobooks.com

abdobooks.com

Printed in the United States of America, North Mankato, Minnesota
092019
012020

Cover Photo: Shutterstock Images
Interior Photos: Shutterstock Images, 1; Nido Huebl/Shutterstock Images, 4–5, 45; Gagliardi Photography/Shutterstock Images, 7; Rainer Lesniewski/Shutterstock Images, 9; Lisa Rapko/Shutterstock Images, 10–11; North Wind Picture Archives, 13, 15, 23; Everett Historical/Shutterstock Images, 18–19, 43; Red Line Editorial, 25; Hans von Nolde/AP Images, 28–29; Marty Lederhandler/AP Images, 34–35; Shawn Baldwin/AP Images, 36; FashionStock.com/Shutterstock Images, 39

Editor: Maddie Spalding
Series Designer: Claire Vanden Branden

Library of Congress Control Number: 2019942113

Publisher's Cataloging-in-Publication Data

Names: Ventura, Marne, author.
Title: New York City / by Marne Ventura
Description: Minneapolis, Minnesota : Abdo Publishing, 2020 | Series: Iconic America | Includes online resources and index.
Identifiers: ISBN 9781532190933 (lib. bdg.) | ISBN 9781532176784 (ebook)
Subjects: LCSH: City and town life--New York (State)--New York--Juvenile literature. | Parks--New York (State)--New York--Juvenile literature. | Industries--New York (State)--New York--Juvenile literature. | Architecture--New York (State)--New York--Juvenile literature. | Empire State Building (New York, N.Y.)--Juvenile literature.
Classification: DDC 917.471--dc23

CONTENTS

CHAPTER ONE

THE CITY THAT NEVER SLEEPS

Gavin made his way to the window and looked down. After climbing 354 steps, he was now inside the crown of the Statue of Liberty. He was far above the ground. The tourists below looked tiny.

Gavin gazed out at Upper New York Bay. A white ferry moved across the water. It headed away from Liberty Island. The ferry had brought him to the island from Manhattan a few hours ago. It held many tourists.

The tour guide said that the Statue of Liberty was a gift from the people of France.

Approximately 3.5 million people visit the Statue of Liberty each year.

It was finished in 1884. Then it was shipped to the United States. The Statue of Liberty is just one of many attractions that make New York a popular US city.

PERSPECTIVES

THE BIG APPLE

One of New York City's nicknames is "The Big Apple." Some people say the phrase was first used in 1909. It described the city as an apple on a tree. The apple symbolizes wealth, and the tree symbolizes the surrounding area. The nickname means that the wealth of the state can be found in New York City. It also means that there are many opportunities in the city. The nickname became popular in the 1920s. Today, many people refer to New York City by this name.

BUSY AND DIVERSE

New York City is in the southeast part of New York State. It is located at the mouth of the Hudson River. The city is always busy. Night or day, there are cars on the streets, people on the sidewalks, and shops open for business. One of New York City's nicknames is "The City That Never Sleeps."

Central Park is an 840-acre (340-ha) park in Manhattan. There, people can boat on a large lake called Central Park Lake.

More than 8 million people live in New York City. The city covers an area of 303 square miles (785 sq km). It has a larger population than any other US city.

New York City is known for its cultural diversity. One in five New Yorkers is an immigrant. By the late 1900s, people from 200 different countries lived in New York City.

Five boroughs make up New York City. They are Manhattan, Brooklyn, the Bronx, Queens, and

THE NEW YORK STOCK EXCHANGE

The New York Stock Exchange opened on Wall Street in 1817. Wall Street runs for about seven blocks from the East River to Broadway. Stockbrokers help people buy and sell stocks at the New York Stock Exchange. Stocks are units of ownership in a company. Investors buy stocks. The company uses the money to operate. When the company makes more money than it spends, it shares the profit with its investors.

Staten Island. The boroughs have different but related histories and cultures. Visitors exploring the city can find a variety of foods, art, and music.

WORLD CENTER

Some of the world's largest banks have offices in New York City. For example, the New York Stock Exchange has been in Manhattan since 1817. Many large companies have headquarters in New York City. For the past 200 years, New York City has been the wealthiest US city.

The city is also a world center for the arts and music. It has nearly 100 museums. Broadway is a famous

NEW YORK CITY MAP

This map shows the five boroughs of New York City. Why are bridges and ferries important for transportation? Why do you think the boroughs are divided up in this way?

area in Manhattan. It has many theaters where actors star in plays and musicals. The city is also famous for its parks, zoos, and holiday parades. These attractions and more draw many people to the city.

CHAPTER TWO

EARLY HISTORY

The first people who settled in present-day Manhattan were Native Americans. They belonged to the Lenni-Lenape tribe. The Lenni-Lenape lived along the North Atlantic coastline as far north as present-day Long Island.

Dutch settlers arrived in the area in the 1600s. They created a colony along the Hudson River in 1624. They called their colony New Netherland. By 1626, the Dutch had created a settlement called New Amsterdam. This settlement was on the south shore of present-day Manhattan. The Lenni-Lenape

A Lenni-Lenape boy dances at the Nanticoke Lenni-Lenape Pow Wow. This gathering is held each year in New Jersey.

were already living in this area. They called it *Manahatta*. In the Lenni-Lenape's Algonquian language, this means "hilly island."

Some people think the settlers purchased Manahatta from the Lenni-Lenape. But historians believe the Lenni-Lenape did not intend to sell their land. The Lenni-Lenape instead thought they were selling the right for the settlers to live on the land with them. But the settlers forced the Lenni-Lenape out of Manahatta.

THE LENNI-LENAPE

The Lenni-Lenape lived throughout the East Coast when the first settlers came from Europe. They had settlements in present-day New Jersey, Delaware, southern New York, and eastern Pennsylvania. In the Lenni-Lenape's native language, the name *Lenni-Lenape* means "Men of Men." Some Lenni-Lenape also translate it as "Original People."

TRADE

At first, the Lenni-Lenape and the settlers got along fairly well. Lenni-Lenape hunters

The Dutch settlers built a canal that ran along present-day Broad Street in Manhattan.

traded furs with the settlers. The settlers gave them beads, tools, and other materials in exchange. But the relationship between the settlers and the Lenni-Lenape soon changed. The settlers took over much of the Lenni-Lenape's lands. The settlers also carried diseases. They were immune to these diseases and not affected by them. But the Lenni-Lenape had never been exposed to the diseases. Many died.

LIFE IN THE COLONY

In 1626, Dutch settlers brought 11 enslaved Africans to New Amsterdam. Over time, the Dutch captured and enslaved more African people. They forced enslaved people to farm, clear lands, and build houses.

Peter Stuyvesant was the governor of New Netherland from 1646 to 1664. He was not popular with the settlers. When the Duke of York sent a British fleet to take over New Amsterdam, the Dutch colonists refused to fight for Stuyvesant. He surrendered in 1664. New Amsterdam was renamed New York City in honor of the duke. The surrounding colony was called the New York colony. British governors began to rule over the colony.

New York City became a trading hub. Many merchants came to New York Harbor. They transported products from the surrounding colonies through the

Many Dutch colonists thought Peter Stuyvesant, *middle*, was too controlling.

harbor on their way to Europe. By 1700, New York City's population had grown to nearly 7,000 people.

THE REVOLUTIONARY WAR

The British established other colonies in the 1700s. By 1770, there were 13 British colonies in what would later become the United States. British rulers taxed the colonists. Many colonists thought the taxes were unfair. They wanted independence. In 1775, war broke out between the colonists and those who remained loyal to Great Britain. This conflict was called the Revolutionary War (1775–1783).

Representatives from the colonies approved a document called the Declaration of Independence on July 4, 1776. The document declared the 13 colonies independent from Great Britain. These colonies, including New York State, became the United States of America.

PERSPECTIVES

SLAVERY IN COLONIAL NEW YORK

In the late 1700s, enslaved Africans made up 20 percent of New York's population. More than 10,000 African Americans lived in New York City. American general George Washington enslaved hundreds of Africans. He used the condition of enslaved people to argue for the colonists' freedom. He warned that colonists who did not resist British rule would become "as tame and abject slaves as the blacks we rule over with such arbitrary sway."

In August 1776, British soldiers invaded New York City. The colonists, led by commander George Washington, fought back. But they were defeated. The British held New York City for seven years.

The colonists won the war in 1783. They reclaimed New York from the British. In 1785, New York City became the nation's capital. The city served as the seat of government until 1790. Then Philadelphia became the US capital. New York City's population quickly grew. It became the largest US city.

EXPLORE ONLINE

Chapter Two discusses the Lenni-Lenape's connection to New York. The article at the website below gives more information about the Lenni-Lenape. How is the information from the website the same as the information in Chapter Two? What new information did you learn from the website?

THE LENAPE

abdocorelibrary.com/new-york-city

CHAPTER THREE

THE 1800s

New York City continued to grow throughout the 1800s. In 1811, officials created a street grid system for Manhattan. They used the grid map to plan the area's expansion. They marked out streets and spaces for parks. The grid system also made the island easier to navigate.

In 1817, work began on the Erie Canal in New York State. It was finished in 1825. The canal is a 363-mile (584-km) waterway. It connects the Atlantic Ocean with the Great Lakes by way of the Hudson River. The canal brought more people, business, and money to the city.

More settlers came to New York after the Erie Canal opened in 1825.

Immigrants from Ireland, Germany, Italy, eastern Europe, and China came to New York in the 1800s. They brought new languages, cultures, and ideas. New York City was home to many activists. Antislavery activists hid enslaved people to help them escape to freedom. Women fought for equal rights, including the right to vote. The first women's rights convention in the United States took place in Seneca Falls, New York, in 1848. It was known as the Seneca Falls Convention.

THE CIVIL WAR

In the mid-1800s, states were divided on the issue of slavery. Southern states wanted to keep slavery. In the North, many people wanted to abolish slavery.

By 1861, 11 southern states had seceded, or separated, from the Union. They formed the Confederacy. Confederate states allowed slavery. Northern states remained part of the Union and followed President Abraham Lincoln. Disagreements between the Union and the Confederacy led to the American Civil War (1861–1865).

New York State was part of the Union. Not all New Yorkers were happy about this. Before the Civil War broke out, southerners had brought cotton to New York City. Cotton was valuable. Confederate states stopped trading in the North during the war. Some New Yorkers wanted to secede from the Union so they could keep trading with the South. Others were involved in the illegal slave trade. Slavery had been outlawed in New York in 1827. But some people continued to illegally buy and sell enslaved Africans.

WALL STREET

New York City's Wall Street gets its name from an actual wall. In 1653, Dutch settlers made enslaved Africans build a wall in this area. The wall's purpose was to protect Dutch settlers from Native American raids. The area later played a key role in the slave trade. In 1711, a slave market was set up on Wall Street. People bought and sold Africans as slaves in this market.

THE DRAFT RIOT

On September 22, 1862, Lincoln issued the Emancipation Proclamation. He declared all enslaved people in the Confederate states to be free. This order went into effect on January 1, 1863. Many freed slaves left the South to settle in the North.

New York City was home to many Irish immigrants. Black people coming into the city were desperate for work. Job competition created tensions between Irish and African American workers.

By 1863, Lincoln realized more soldiers would be needed for the Union to win the war. He created a military draft. Male citizens between the ages of 20 and 45 were required to enlist. They could be called up to fight for the Union. But men could pay a large sum to avoid being drafted. They could also hire others to fight for them. Many rich men bought their way out of the draft. Black men could not be drafted because they

Rioters burned down an African American orphanage in the 1863 New York City draft riots. The 233 children in the building managed to escape.

were not citizens. Many poor immigrants found this system unfair.

The draft took effect on July 11. On July 13, a riot broke out in New York City. Thousands of white workers

PERSPECTIVES

THE TRIANGLE SHIRTWAIST FIRE

In the late 1800s and early 1900s, immigrants had limited employment opportunities. They often accepted whatever jobs they could find. Employers usually paid them very little money. Immigrants often worked 15 to 18 hours each day. In 1911, a fire broke out on the top floors of the Triangle Shirtwaist factory in New York City. The factory employed many immigrant women. Factory owners kept the building's exit doors locked. Workers could not escape. Of the 500 people working in the factory, 146 died. This tragedy made the US government realize that better workplace safety laws were needed.

attacked military and government buildings. Most of the rioters were Irish immigrants. They attacked soldiers and policemen. They also targeted black residents. They set fire to 50 buildings. The riot lasted four days. Historians estimate that the rioters killed between 100 and 1,000 people.

BOOMING BUSINESS

The Union won the Civil War in 1865.

ELLIS ISLAND
IMMIGRANTS

This graph shows the number of immigrants who passed through New York's Ellis Island immigration station in certain years from its opening in 1892 to 1920. How did the number of immigrants change in these years? What do you think may be some reasons for these changes?

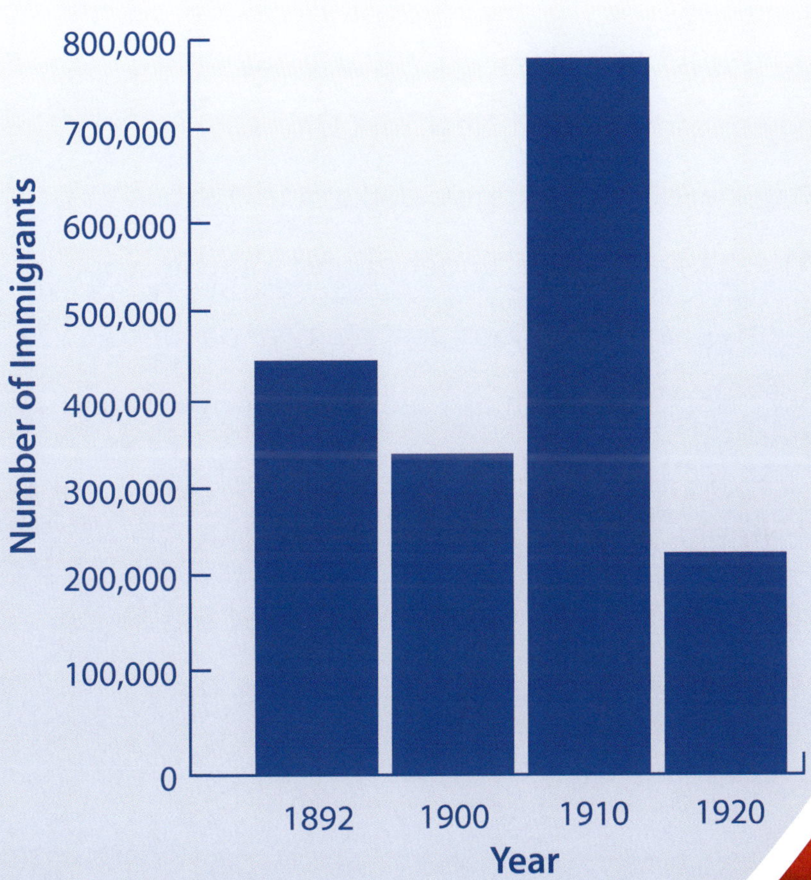

The states were once again united. Slavery was outlawed throughout the country.

In the late 1800s, New York City's population increased. Ellis Island became the entry point for immigrants in 1892. This immigration station was in Upper New York Bay.

In 1898, New York City's borders were expanded. The five boroughs were created from surrounding areas. They became part of New York City. City leaders oversaw the building of bridges, parks, and a subway system. The subway was an underground train network. Construction sites offered jobs as the city expanded. The city was also home to many factories. People found jobs at these factories. But the working conditions in these factories were poor. Some factory workers created labor unions. Labor unions fought for better working conditions.

STRAIGHT TO THE SOURCE

New York poet Emma Lazarus wrote a poem about the Statue of Liberty. The poem begins:

Here at our sea-washed, sunset gates shall stand

A mighty woman with a torch, whose flame

Is the imprisoned lightning, and her name

Mother of Exiles. From her beacon-hand

Glows world-wide welcome; her mild eyes command

The air-bridged harbor that twin cities frame.

"Keep, ancient lands, your storied pomp!" cries she

With silent lips. "Give me your tired, your poor,

Your huddled masses yearning to breathe free."

Source: Emma Lazarus. "The New Colossus." *Emma Lazarus: Selected Poems and Other Writings*. Ontario, Canada: Broadview Press, 2002. Print. 233.

Consider Your Audience

Read this poem carefully. Rewrite the poem in your own words so that a younger sibling or friend could understand it.

CHAPTER FOUR

THE 1900s

In the early 1900s, many African Americans left the South to escape discrimination and violence. They were also drawn to better employment opportunities in the North. Those who came to New York City settled in a district called Harlem. Many were artists, musicians, or writers. They ushered in a cultural movement called the Harlem Renaissance. Black arts and culture flourished.

New York City's Jewish population also increased in the early 1900s. Between 1880 and 1920, this population grew from approximately 80,000 to 1.5 million people. Most Jewish immigrants came from central and

A couple dances at the Savoy Ballroom in Harlem in the 1950s. New styles of dance were invented during the Harlem Renaissance.

eastern Europe. They found more freedom and religious acceptance in the United States.

THE GREAT DEPRESSION

On October 29, 1929, the stock market crashed. Investors lost $14 billion on the New York Stock Exchange. This day became known as Black Tuesday. The Great Depression followed. This was a period of high unemployment and poverty. It lasted until the late 1930s.

Franklin D. Roosevelt was the US president at the time. He started a program called the New Deal. This program created jobs. Some workers built New York City's Central

THE EMPIRE STATE BUILDING

In 1930, workers began to build a large skyscraper in Manhattan. It was called the Empire State Building. This construction project was not part of the New Deal program, but it employed many people. Approximately 3,400 workers built the skyscraper. The Empire State Building is 1,454 feet (443 m) tall. When it was completed in 1931, it was the world's tallest skyscraper.

Park Zoo. Others helped build the Lincoln Tunnel. This tunnel runs underneath the Hudson River.

CHANGES AND CHALLENGES

In some ways, New York City became more developed after World War II (1939–1945). For example, construction began on the United Nations (UN) headquarters building in Manhattan in 1948. The UN addresses human rights issues.

Despite these positive changes, there were problems within the city. Major industries left New York City after the war. Many people lived in poverty. In addition, there were racial divides. Some property deeds said that homeowners could not sell their homes to people of color. This prevented black people from living in white neighborhoods. Black people also had to pay higher interest rates on home loans. This made it difficult for many African Americans to afford houses.

By 1950, nearly 190,000 Puerto Ricans had settled in New York City. The city's African American population

PERSPECTIVES

THE STONEWALL RIOTS

By the 1960s, a few gay bars had been established in New York City. People who were gay or who had other identities not accepted by society gathered in these bars. They found support and acceptance in these places. But police often raided gay bars. This happened in New York City's Stonewall Inn on June 28, 1969. Police beat up and arrested some people in the bar. This injustice angered many people. In response, they rioted. The Stonewall Riots attracted national attention. Today, the Stonewall Inn remains a reminder of New York City's role in the gay rights movement.

also increased during this time. There was not enough housing available for the city's growing population.

As the population grew, highways were built and expanded. Highways allowed people to easily get from the suburbs to the city. Most of the people who lived in the suburbs were white. They had moved out of neighborhoods in the city when people of color had moved in.

CIVIL RIGHTS

In the 1950s and 1960s, many African Americans protested racial discrimination and violence. These decades were the height of the American civil rights movement. Black activists organized demonstrations. One such demonstration took place in New York City. On February 3, 1964, more than 460,000 students and teachers skipped classes. New York City's schools were racially segregated. Students and teachers wanted to bring attention to this issue. Their protest was one of the largest civil rights demonstrations of the 1960s.

FURTHER EVIDENCE

Chapter Four discusses New York City's African American history. What was one of the main points of this chapter? What key evidence supports this point? Read the article at the website below. Does the information on the website support this point? Or does it present new evidence?

BLACK NEW YORKERS

abdocorelibrary.com/new-york-city

CHAPTER FIVE

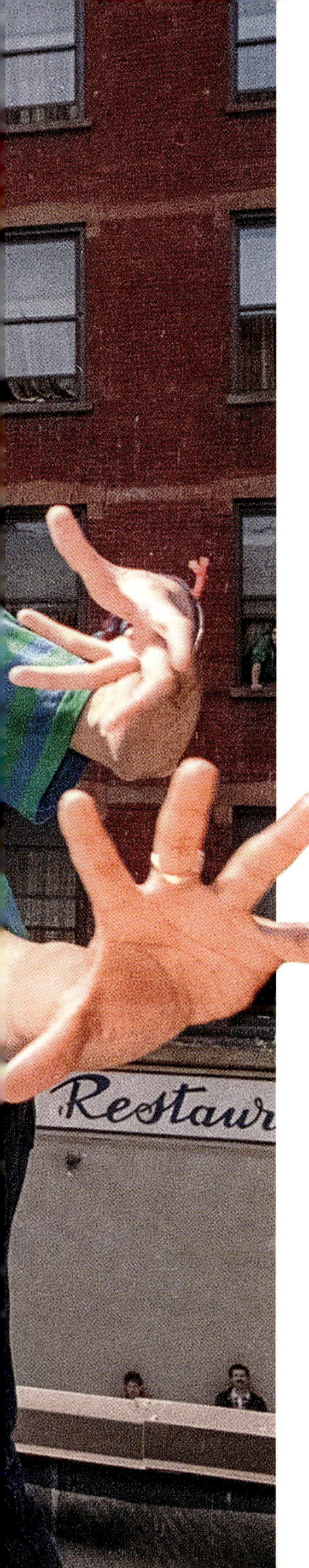

THE CITY'S INFLUENCE

The civil rights movement paved the way for other cultural movements. In the 1970s and 1980s, rap and hip-hop music emerged in New York City. A highway had been built through the Bronx. The highway displaced many black and Hispanic people who had lived in this borough. These people felt ignored. Many of them expressed their feelings through music and art. The hip-hop movement involved music, dancing, and art. Young people spray painted graffiti throughout the city as a form of self-expression.

Run-DMC and the Beastie Boys were popular hip-hop groups in the 1980s.

Firefighters put out fires and searched for survivors after the September 11 attacks. More than 300 firefighters died.

New York City continued to expand throughout the late 1990s. Then on September 11, 2001, tragedy struck. Islamist terrorists hijacked four airplanes. One plane was crashed into the Pentagon. The Pentagon is the US military's headquarters in Arlington, Virginia. Another plane crashed into a field in Pennsylvania. Terrorists crashed the other planes into two skyscrapers called the Twin Towers. The Twin Towers were in the World Trade Center, a building complex in New

York City's Financial District. They were destroyed in the attack. Nearly 3,000 people were killed. It was the deadliest terrorist attack in US history. More than 400 police officers, firefighters, and other first responders died.

The terrorists hijacked the planes in response to US military involvement in Muslim-majority countries. They supported a violent extremist version of Islam. Most Muslim Americans did not agree with their actions.

The site of the World Trade Center attack was named Ground Zero. New York officials constructed a new building on the site. It includes a memorial and museum dedicated to the victims of the September 11 attacks. A skyscraper called One World Trade Center stands next to the memorial and museum. It opened in 2014. It is the tallest building in the United States.

HURRICANE SANDY

The stock market and the banking industry took a downturn in the early 2000s. The economy was on the upswing in 2012. Then Hurricane Sandy swept through New York City. It caused $19 billion in damages. The subway and tunnels flooded. Power systems failed. Fires broke out in Queens. They burned more than 100 homes to the ground.

Hurricane Sandy was not the first tropical storm to hit the city. Since the 1800s, many hurricanes have damaged the city. New York State is on the coastline of the Atlantic Ocean. Hurricanes travel across oceans.

PERSPECTIVES

OCCUPY WALL STREET

In 2011, a movement called Occupy Wall Street began in Manhattan. Approximately 1,000 people gathered near Wall Street on September 17. They protested economic inequality. They were frustrated with the growing gap between the rich and the poor. They thought financial companies contributed to these problems. Today, activists continue to raise awareness of these issues. One major cause they support is increasing minimum wages. The minimum wage is the lowest amount employers are required to pay their workers.

Hurricane Sandy flooded coastal communities in New York, including Brooklyn.

Scientists are studying how climate change will affect New York in the future. Climate change is a shift in global climate patterns. Scientists predict that by 2050, severe weather will be more common. Scientists and city leaders are working to help the city prepare.

GLOBAL INFLUENCE

New York City remains a diverse and active city. Immigrants continue to influence the city's cultures and cuisines. Visitors to the city can find Greek, Turkish, Korean, and many other varieties of foods.

New York City chefs, designers, and other leaders in their fields have international influence. New York Fashion Week takes place in Manhattan. This event happens twice each year. Designers introduce the latest clothing trends. New York City is also home to some of the world's best music schools. And many professional sports leagues are based in the city. For these reasons, people all over the world recognize New York as an iconic American city.

BASEBALL

The first formal baseball club was created in New York City. A group of men founded the Knickerbocker Base Ball Club in 1845. Over time, the men established the rules for baseball. Baseball became popular during the Civil War. Some reports claim that Union soldiers played baseball with Confederate soldiers during the war. Today, New York City has two Major League Baseball teams: the New York Yankees and the New York Mets.

STRAIGHT TO THE SOURCE

Brian Rashid is a writer for *Forbes* magazine. He first came to New York City when he was 22 years old. He wrote about his opinion of the city:

> *No one looks the same. I went to college at a University where everyone looked like me. The same was true for my high school. The opposite is true in NYC. No one looks the same. It makes you question everything you ever thought and learned. It makes you curious. It makes you wonder, where are these people coming from and going? What do they care about? How can I help them? These are the same questions that make a business successful or a life fulfilling.*

Source: Brian Rashid. "Why Everyone Should Live In New York City." *Forbes*. Forbes, September 2, 2015. Web. Accessed March 8, 2019.

What's the Big Idea?

Take a close look at this passage. What is the main point Rashid is making about the people in New York City? How do you think the attitudes of the city's residents shape the city as a whole?

IMPORTANT DATES

1626

The Dutch create a settlement in the colony of New Netherland. The settlement is on the south shore of present-day Manhattan. The Dutch call it New Amsterdam. They push out Lenni-Lenape people who had lived in the area for more than 9,000 years.

1664

English settlers take over New Netherland. They rename it New York in honor of the Duke of York. They rename New Amsterdam, calling it New York City.

1825

The Erie Canal is completed. It brings more people and goods into the city.

1898

The five boroughs merge to form modern-day New York City.

1929–late 1930s

Many of New York City's residents are jobless during the Great Depression.

1969

The Stonewall Riots protest police violence at gay bars.

1970s–1980s
Hip-hop music takes off in the Bronx.

September 11, 2001
Terrorists destroy the Twin Towers of the World Trade Center and kill nearly 3,000 people.

2014
The One World Trade Center skyscraper opens on the site of the September 11 terrorist attack.

STOP AND THINK

Tell the Tale

Chapter One of this book describes a visit to the Statue of Liberty. Imagine you are visiting New York City for the first time. Which of the places mentioned in Chapter One would you like to visit? Write 200 words about your planned trip. Describe the places and sites you plan to see.

Surprise Me

Chapter Two discusses the early history of New York City. After reading this book, what two or three facts about the city's early history did you find most surprising? Write a few sentences about each fact. Why did you find each fact surprising?

Say What?

Studying a city and its history can mean learning a lot of new vocabulary. Find five words in this book you've never heard before. Use a dictionary to find out what they mean. Then write the meanings in your own words, and use each word in a new sentence.

Take a Stand

Many New York City residents say it is the best city in the world. They say the crowds of people, the diversity, and the city's many attractions make it the perfect place to live. Do you think you would like to live in New York City? Or would you rather just visit? What are the pros and cons of living in the city?

GLOSSARY

abolish
to formally end something

borough
a part of a city that has its own government

colony
land owned by a faraway country or nation

culture
the social customs, beliefs, and traits of a particular group of people

discrimination
the unjust treatment of a person or group based on race or other perceived differences

diversity
the state of having people of different races and backgrounds together in one place

draft
a call by a government to serve in the military

immigrant
a person who leaves his or her homeland to make a home in a different country

segregate
to separate people of different races or ethnic groups through separate schools and other public spaces

terrorist
someone who uses violence to threaten a group of people

ONLINE RESOURCES

To learn more about New York City, visit our free resource websites below.

Visit **abdocorelibrary.com** or scan this QR code for free Common Core resources for teachers and students, including vetted activities, multimedia, and booklinks, for deeper subject comprehension.

Visit **abdobooklinks.com** or scan this QR code for free additional online weblinks for further learning. These links are routinely monitored and updated to provide the most current information available.

LEARN MORE

Hamilton, John. *New York: The Empire State*. Minneapolis, MN: Abdo Publishing, 2017.

Lanier, Wendy H. *Life during the Great Depression*. Minneapolis, MN: Abdo Publishing, 2015.

INDEX

About the Author

Marne Ventura has written more than 100 books for children. A former elementary school teacher, she holds a master's degree in education from the University of California. Her favorite subjects are history, science, food, arts and crafts, and the lives of creative people. Marne and her husband live on the central coast of California.